LANICE LAWRENCE

31 Days of Prayer, Purpose, and
Power for Kingdom Entrepreneurs

FAITH *to* BUILD

Copyright © Lanice Lawrence 2025

All rights reserved. No part of this publication may be reproduced, stored in a retrieval system, or transmitted in any form or by any means, electronic, mechanical, photocopying, recording, or otherwise, without written permission of the author or publisher.

ISBN: 979-8-9994882-0-6

For permission to reproduce excerpts, use copyrighted material, translate, or adapt this work, please contact the author or publisher.

Disclaimer

This devotional is intended to provide inspiration, encouragement, and general information based on the author's personal experiences and insights in business, finance, and faith. It is not intended to serve as legal, financial, tax, or other professional advice.

Readers are strongly encouraged to seek personalized guidance from qualified professionals—such as licensed tax advisors, accountants, attorneys, or financial planners—before making decisions related to business structure, tax planning, or financial management.

While the strategies and principles shared are meant to empower Kingdom-minded entrepreneurs, each individual's circumstances are unique. The author and publisher disclaim any liability for outcomes resulting from actions taken based on the content of this book.

Faith and business are both journeys. Walk in wisdom, seek godly counsel, and above all—seek God in all things.

Although every effort has been made to ensure the accuracy of the information provided, laws and regulations may change. The author and publisher make no guarantees and accept no responsibility for errors, omissions, or outcomes resulting from the use of this material.

Faith to Build

Endorsement

*"Wisdom is the principal thing;
therefore get wisdom: and with all thy getting get understanding."*

– Proverbs 4:7

What a joy and honor it is to endorse this powerful devotional by Lanice Lawrence. She has done an exceptional job of compiling wisdom, insight, and encouragement to uplift and empower others—especially those called to the marketplace. As a woman who has faithfully walked the journey of entrepreneurship, Lanice offers more than words—she offers experience, faith, and purpose.

Faith to Build is a must-read for anyone aspiring to walk in wisdom and step fully into their role as a Kingdom Entrepreneur. This devotional invites leaders to dig deeper, seek God's face, and align their business journey with His divine will. In the midst of life's demands, it provides a sacred space to pause, reflect, and allow God to move in and through your business.

As you read each entry, I encourage you to pray, journal, and remain open to the leading of the Holy Spirit. I believe you'll experience divine clarity, strategy, and breakthroughs that will not only impact your business but leave a lasting legacy.

May your faith be strengthened, your vision expanded, and your business prospered through this life-changing devotional.

— **Dr. Paulus Taylor**
Senior Pastor
Trinity Community Church
Hartford, CT, USA

As a first-generation college graduate and new business owner, I often feel like I'm building from scratch — with no blueprint. Faith to Build reminded me that I am the blueprint. Lanice's transparency about her own journey gave me courage. Her 'Legacy Letter to My Children' brought me to tears. The devotionals are sharp, anointed, and actionable. This book is not only for today's entrepreneur, but for generations to come.

— **Kevin Lawrence**
First-Gen College Grad & Business Owner

If you're a Kingdom entrepreneur looking to blend faith with focus, Faith to Build is a must-have for your journey. I felt so inspired, empowered and reminded that yes, I really do have the faith to build what God gave me.

From the very first page, you can tell this is more than just a book; it's a whole blueprint for visionaries who know their business is more than a hustle. It's a divine assignment.

What I love most is that it doesn't stop at spiritual encouragement. Lanice gives you strategy, financial wisdom, and tools you can actually use. Irrespective of where you are in your process, this devotional reminds you that you're not building alone. God is the architect.

This is a business gem that just hits differently. Each day feels like a download from heaven and a coaching session in one.

Thank you for writing this. You didn't just give us a devotional — you gave us direction. May every reader be just as inspired.

— **Min. Saneka Nelson, She is a Testimony**

This 31-day devotional journey is more than just inspiration — it's a strategic blueprint for Kingdom entrepreneurs. Each day blends scripture, business wisdom, and prayer in a way that's practical and spirit-led.

Whether you're launching a business or just trying to keep the faith while juggling real life, this book meets you right where you are. Lanice writes with authenticity and clarity, reminding us that building a business with God is not only possible — it's powerful!

Highly recommend for every visionary who's ever felt like they had to separate faith and business. This devotion reminds you to build boldly — with God as your CEO.

— **Nickeisha Bewry-Clarke, LNHA, MHA, BSN, RN**

Faith to Build

Foreword

Faith to Build is more than a devotional — it's a powerful blueprint for purpose-driven entrepreneurs who are building with God.

Written by an author who has walked the journey, faced uncertainty, and witnessed firsthand the miraculous results of building by faith, this 31-day guide offers both inspiration and instruction for those ready to align their business with their Kingdom calling.

Each day delivers:

- A powerful, Word-based theme that speaks directly to visionaries
- Heart-stirring devotionals that encourage and ignite faith
- Strategy Tips for clarity in structure, marketing, and expansion
- Practical Tips grounded in real-world experience and sound wisdom
- Purpose Notes to help you stay anchored to your God-given assignment
- And prayers that invite divine direction, favor, and protection

Minister Lanice Lawrence wants readers to recognize that *Faith to Build* empowers one to dream big, act wisely, and lead courageously. Whether you are launching, scaling, or starting again, this life-transformative devotional will equip you to trust your gift, walk in your God-given authority, and build what God has entrusted to you.

At the end of these 31 days, the author invites us to activate what we've built and rise with clarity, confidence, and a Kingdom mindset. Every prayer, principle, and page are carefully designed to equip us not just to dream, but to do. Now is your time to build with intention, lead with boldness, and move with faith.

This devotional is the vehicle to your next level!

> *"Have faith in God... whatever you ask for in prayer, believe that you have received it, and it will be yours."*
>
> — Mark 11:22, 24 (NIV)

— *Minister Carol Pusey, MDiv., BCC*

FAITH TO BUILD

31 Days of Prayer, Purpose & Power for Kingdom Entrepreneurs

*Your blueprint for building a business
rooted in faith and aligned with God's purpose.*

Building a business by faith takes more than big dreams—it requires vision, spiritual discipline, and strategy. *Faith to Build* is a 31-day devotional designed for entrepreneurs who know their business is part of a greater Kingdom assignment.

Each day combines scripture, prophetic insight, and real-life business wisdom to help you build with boldness, lead with integrity, and grow with excellence. Inside, you'll find:

- A daily theme grounded in the Word of God
- Heartfelt devotionals that speak to the soul of a visionary
- Strategy Tips to guide decisions in business structure, marketing, and growth
- Practical Tips rooted in proven financial and operational principles
- Purpose Notes to keep your heart aligned with your assignment
- Prayers that invite God's wisdom, favor, and covering over your journey

This is more than a devotional—it's a blueprint. Whether you're launching, scaling, or rebuilding, Faith to Build equips you to walk in authority, trust your gift, and steward your calling with clarity and courage.

BONUS: Kingdom Builder's Business Toolkit

Includes actionable worksheets and templates on:

- Business formation, structure, and compliance
- Tax planning, bookkeeping systems, and key financial statement
- Retirement savings strategies and credit-building guidance
- Legacy planning, asset protection, and financial safeguards

Who This Is For

- Christian entrepreneurs launching or scaling a business
- Visionaries who want to blend faith with financial strategy
- Men and women called to impact the marketplace with integrity
- Kingdom builders who want to disrupt culture, create wealth, and leave legacy

How to Use This Devotional

- Dedicate 10–15 minutes each day for scripture, reflection, and strategy
- Journal your insights, wins, and divine downloads
- Use the Legacy Vision Worksheet to clarify your purpose
- Revisit chapters, prayers, and worksheets as your business evolves

Build boldly. Lead with faith. Grow with wisdom.

You have Faith to Build—now build what God has entrusted to you.

PREFACE

Why I Wrote This Devotional

When I started my business, I didn't realize I was stepping into ministry.

I thought I was just trying to make ends meet. But over time, I began to see that my spreadsheets were sermons, my systems were seeds, and every client I served was part of a greater Kingdom assignment.

What I once viewed as a side hustle became God's vehicle to provide, heal, restore, and multiply—not just for me, but for my family and for every life connected to my obedience.

I wrote this devotional for visionaries—men and women who feel that same pull. For those who know they're called to build, not just for profit, but with purpose. You're building with prayer in one hand and strategy in the other. You desire increase, but not at the expense of integrity. You want to leave a legacy that reflects both faith and excellence.

This is more than motivation. This is revelation. It's a daily guide for Kingdom entrepreneurs who want to align their faith with their business decisions and walk in divine instruction.

Inside these 31 days, you'll find:

- A daily theme grounded in God's Word
- Strategic insight to grow your business in alignment with Kingdom principles
- Practical tips I've personally applied in building a profitable firm
- A prayer to keep your heart aligned with your assignment
- Bonus worksheets, financial tools, and checklists to help you apply what you learn

My prayer is that this book becomes both your blueprint and your mirror—a reflection of what's possible when faith leads and obedience follows.

Let's build together.

— Lanice Lawrence

INTRODUCTION

Welcome to Your 31-Day Journey

Welcome to *Faith to Build* — a 31-day devotional designed to ignite your faith, fuel your purpose, and empower your entrepreneurial walk with Kingdom insight. This is more than a business guide. It's a spiritual blueprint for visionary leaders who are building with God at the center.

Whether you're just getting started or scaling with strategy, this devotional will anchor you in prayer, refine your perspective, and position you to grow with clarity, boldness, and divine wisdom.

This journey is broken into weekly themes to help you build momentum—spiritually, mentally, financially, and structurally:

Week 1: Days 1–5 — Laying the Foundation: Vision, Prayer, and Wisdom

Answer the call to build with clarity. This week centers on vision, divine direction, and establishing a strong spiritual foundation.

Week 2: Days 6–10 — Provision, Obedience, and Excellence

Trust God's provision and walk in obedience. Learn how excellence is birthed from alignment, not just effort.

Week 3: Days 11–15 — Structure, Finances, and Faith

Strengthen the foundation with structure and stewardship. Explore systems, finances, and how faith fuels both.

Week 4: Days 16–20 — Expansion, Branding, and Breaking Cycles

You were created for impact. These devotionals guide you in expanding your reach, branding with purpose, and breaking generational limitations.

Week 5: Days 21–25 — Credit, Protection, and Divine Favor

God uses both spiritual and practical resources to fund vision. Focus on wise credit usage, protection of the vision, and walking in divine favor.

Week 6: Days 26–30 — Balance, Breakthrough, and Legacy

Lead from a place of rest and wisdom. Learn to steward time, pursue breakthrough, and build a lasting legacy.

Day 31 — Fully Surrendered, Fully Empowered

True power is found in full surrender. As you release control to God, expect renewed peace, strategy, and elevation for the next level.

Afterword: Activate What You Built

Now that you've completed your 31-day journey, continue to build with intention and faith. At the end of this devotional, you'll find:

- A Bold Victory Statement to declare over your life and business
- Bonus Worksheets to apply what you've learned and track your growth

You're not just a business owner—you are a Kingdom builder. Let this be your season to build boldly, lead with purpose, and walk fully empowered.

Let's build. Faith first.

Faith to Build

Dedication Page

To my loving mother, Sharon — your tireless work ethic, steadfast faith, and constant support have been my refuge and strength. Through your example, I've learned resilience in hard work and grace in every challenge. Thank you for being the foundation of who I am.

To my beloved husband, Raphael — my steadfast partner and greatest encourager. Your unwavering support and love have carried me through every doubt. Thank you for believing in me when I struggled to believe in myself.

To my precious twin daughters, Jalissa and Larissa — your laughter brightens my days, and your future inspires every sacrifice I make. May you always know your worth and walk boldly in your God-given destiny.

To my four strong sons, Jahiem, Jameel, Michael-Joshua, and Raphael — each of you holds a unique purpose. I pray that the legacy I build today becomes the launching pad for your greatest achievements.

This book is dedicated to all of you — my family, the reason I rise each morning with purpose. It is also for every parent, every first-generation trailblazer, and every Kingdom entrepreneur daring to dream bigger, build smarter, and leave a legacy that transcends generations.

May these pages inspire you to trust the process, walk boldly in faith, and know that with God's guidance, what you start today will multiply beyond measure.

With all my love and faith,

Lanice Lawrence

Faith to Build

Table of Contents

Faith to Build — My Yes Became the Blueprint 1

Legacy Letter to My Children 3

Letter to the Reader You Are Not Alone 5

DAY 1: The Call to Build The Blueprint Begins with Obedience 7

Day 2: The Foundation of Prayer 11

DAY 3: Purpose Over Profit 13

DAY 4: Invest in Wisdom 15

DAY 5: Trusting God's Timing 19

DAY 6: Provision for the Vision 23

DAY 7: The Cost of Obedience 27

DAY 8 Building Generational Wealth 29

DAY 9: Resting While Building 31

DAY 10: Excellence Reflects the Kingdom 35

DAY 11: The Right Structure 37

DAY 12: Building with Integrity 41

DAY 13: When to Pivot or Persevere 45

DAY 14: Attracting the Right Clients 49

DAY 15: Pricing with Confidence 53

DAY 16: Overcoming Comparison 57

DAY 17: Networking with Kingdom Purpose 59

DAY 18: Spirit-Led Branding 61

DAY 19: Multiplication & Expansion 65

DAY 20: Credit as Kingdom Capital 69

DAY 21: Hiring with Discernment 71

DAY 22: Stewarding Wealth Wisely 75

DAY 23: Protecting the Vision 79

DAY 24: Becoming a Blessing 83

DAY 25: Walking in Favor 85

DAY 26: Time Management & Balance 87

DAY 27: Financial Breakthroughs 91

DAY 28: Standing Out in the Market 93

DAY 29: Leaving a Legacy 97

DAY 30: Fully Surrendered, Fully Empowered 99

DAY 31: Celebrating Wins God's Way 101

FAITH TO BUILD DECLARATION 105

Bonus Section Kingdom Builder's Business Toolkit 107

Legacy Planning, Asset Protection & Financial Safeguards Worksheet 113

Legacy Vision Worksheet 115

Business Credit Starter Steps Worksheet 119

Profit & Loss Worksheet 121

Bonus Resource 123

Resources & References 127

Disclaimer 129

About the Author 131

Acknowledgements 133

Faith to Build — My Yes Became the Blueprint

I didn't come from wealth. I didn't inherit a business plan or legacy.

I am the blueprint.

I'm a first-generation college graduate, a wife, a mother of six, and a believer who once juggled a full-time job, a side business, and the weight of motherhood—while living paycheck to paycheck. I was tired, overwhelmed, and silently pouring from an empty cup. I gave everything to everyone and left almost nothing for myself.

But even in the chaos, I felt a divine pull—a holy dissatisfaction. I knew I wasn't created just to survive. God was calling me to something greater. Not just to earn—but to establish. Not just to work—but to build.

I didn't have investors, mentors, or free time. But I had faith to build. I had a vision from God and a "yes" in my spirit—and that yes changed everything.

With trembling faith, I walked away from my full-time job as an Accountant and turned my part-time hustle into a **thriving accounting and tax firm**—*a firm that now provides steady income, retirement contributions, life insurance, and generational opportunity for my family. Today, my company creates jobs, protects legacies, and empowers other entrepreneurs to do the same.*

Through my firm, I've helped clients restructure their businesses, recover from financial mistakes, reduce tax burdens, and turn what looked like debt into destiny. We don't just manage numbers—we build futures with strategy, structure, and stewardship.

God gave me strategy when I lacked direction. Strength when I was weary. Provision when I had nothing but vision. He taught me to lead with integrity, serve with excellence, and build something that would outlive me.

Now, I help Kingdom entrepreneurs shift from survival to stewardship, from hustle to legacy—not because I had it all figured out, but because I said yes and built by faith.

This devotional was birthed from that yes.

It's for the tired parent.

The late-night visionary.

The man or woman determined to break generational curses and build generational wealth.

The entrepreneur who wants to glorify God through their business and leave a legacy that their children can build on, not start over.

This book is for you.

*Each day is anchored in **scripture, strategy, and Spirit-led insight**. As you walk through these 31 days, expect **clarity, confidence, and divine direction**. **Chains will break. Vision will sharpen. Faith will rise.***

"Unless the Lord builds the house, the builders labor in vain…" — Psalm 127:1

You're not just building a business.
You're building by faith.
You're building with wisdom.
You're building a legacy.

Let's build—with bold faith, divine strategy, and the power of God.

— Lanice Lawrence

Legacy Letter to My Children

My dear Jalissa, Larissa, Jahiem, Jameel, Michael-Joshua, and Raphael,

I am writing this letter to you as a mother, a believer, and a woman who is determined to build a legacy—not just of wealth, but of faith, purpose, and freedom. I want you to know that every sacrifice I make, every sleepless night, and every challenge I face is because I believe in your future.

I am the first in our family to walk this path—a first-generation college graduate and entrepreneur. That means I am starting from the bottom so that you don't have to. I'm laying the foundation so you can build higher, dream bigger, and live freer.

Remember this: your worth is not measured by dollars or titles but by the faith you carry, the love you give, and the courage you show. Whatever you do, do it with integrity and always honor God. He is the source of every blessing you will receive.

I pray you inherit not just material wealth but the strength to overcome, the wisdom to lead, and the heart to serve. May you continue what I start, and may your legacy be even greater than mine.

Always know I am proud of you, I believe in you, and I am walking this journey with you—in prayer, love, and purpose.

With all my heart,

Mom

Faith to Build

LETTER TO THE READER

You Are Not Alone

Dear Entrepreneur,

If you are reading this, it means you carry a dream deep in your heart—a vision that won't let you rest. Maybe you've been working late nights, juggling responsibilities, or feeling overwhelmed by the weight of your calling. Maybe you wonder if you're enough, if you have what it takes, or if the sacrifices will ever pay off.

I want you to know: **You are not alone.**

Whether you're a mother, a father, a single parent, or someone stepping out for the very first time—God sees you. He hears your prayers, your tears, and your silent cries. He is your partner, your guide, and your provision.

This devotional is designed to remind you that you are part of a divine movement—a community of Kingdom builders who are rewriting their stories and breaking generational chains. It's for those who know their business is more than profit; it's a platform for purpose, a legacy for family, and a testimony for the world.

So take heart. Stand firm. Lean into the prayers and reflections you will find in these pages. Let them strengthen your spirit, sharpen your strategy, and ignite your faith.

You are not alone. You are chosen. You are empowered. And with God's grace, your business will not only survive—it will thrive and multiply.

With faith and encouragement,

Lanice Lawrence

Faith to Build

DAY 1

The Call to Build
The Blueprint Begins with Obedience

Scripture

> *"Then the Lord answered me and said:*
> *'Write the vision and make it plain on tablets,*
> *that he may run who reads it.'"*

— Habakkuk 2:2 (NKJV)

Devotion

God isn't simply calling you to launch a business — He's calling you to build a legacy. That vision stirring in your heart is not just a good idea; it's a divine assignment. Kingdom businesses are born out of obedience, not convenience.

That persistent idea? That gentle tug on your spirit? It's God inviting you to partner with Him. Before the business plan, before the marketing strategy — He asks for your yes. You don't need every detail figured out. What you need is a willing heart.

When you move in faith, God provides the blueprint. Your "yes" is the foundation He will build on — to bless your family, impact lives, and fund Kingdom work.

Reflection

What vision has God entrusted you with that you've delayed or dismissed?

What's holding you back from writing it down and acting on it?

Strategy Tip

Bring structure to your God-given idea. Start with a 1-page vision plan:

- **Who do you serve?**
- **What problem do you solve?**
- **How does your business glorify God?**

Let this simple plan serve as your foundation. Clarity invites momentum—and obedience unlocks provision.

Practical Tip

Register your business name with the Secretary of State and obtain your EIN from the IRS to establish your legal structure.

Purpose Notes

Not ready for an LLC? You can start with a DBA (Doing Business As) and register with your local town or city hall. It offers the same federal tax benefits as an LLC when operating as a sole proprietor. Start where you are—just start legally and with intention.

Prayer

Lord, thank You for trusting me with this vision. I write what You've placed in my heart, knowing it's greater than I can imagine. Give me the courage to obey, even in uncertainty. Help me steward this assignment with boldness and clarity. Let my business reflect Your will, bring You glory, and create lasting impact. I surrender my plans—lead me every step of the way. In Jesus' name, amen.

Faith to Build

DAY 2

The Foundation of Prayer

Scripture

> *"Ask, and it will be given to you;*
> *seek, and you will find; knock, and the door will be opened to you."*
>
> — Matthew 7:7

Devotion

Prayer is the unshakable foundation of every Kingdom entrepreneur's success. It's not a backup plan — it's your boardroom, your strategy hub, and your lifeline to divine instruction. Before sending invoices, launching programs, or hiring team members, prayer should be your **first move**, not your last resort.

When you pray, you're not just speaking — you're aligning. Prayer connects your plans to God's timing, your vision to His wisdom, and your movement to His power. The world may depend on analytics and hustle, but **Kingdom builders operate by revelation**. Prayer removes confusion, activates clarity, and positions you for supernatural results that data alone can't produce.

Your business isn't just a brand—it's a **branch of God's Kingdom** in the marketplace. Through prayer, you don't just grow profit — you cultivate purpose.

Strategy Tip

Start each business day with 5–10 minutes of focused, quiet prayer. Keep a dedicated "Prayer & Strategy" journal to write what God reveals. At the end of the week, review how His insight guided your actions and impacted results.

Practical Tip

Set an alarm or reminder for your prayer time, and create a quiet, distraction-free space for your daily connection with God. Make this a non-negotiable appointment.

Purpose Notes: Kingdom Business Keys

Prayer isn't passive—it's powerful.
Track God's answers like business data.
Revelation outpaces research.
God's guidance is worth the pause.

Prayer

Father, thank You for the gift of prayer. Help me never to build without first seeking Your wisdom. Speak clearly, Lord, and I will listen. Align my business plans with Your perfect will. Amen.

DAY 3

Purpose Over Profit

Scripture

> *"But seek first the kingdom of God and His righteousness, and all these things shall be added to you."*
>
> — Matthew 6:33 (NKJV)

Devotion

Chasing profit without purpose leads to burnout, emptiness, and frustration. But when your business is anchored in the Kingdom and led by God-given purpose, provision follows.

Purpose gives your work meaning. It fuels persistence, attracts the right people, and creates long-term impact. When you prioritize:

- **Impact over income**
- **Service over sales**
- **Legacy over luxury**

God honors your obedience. Your business shifts from simply making money to making ministry moves.

God never designed your business to be just a source of income—it's a tool for influence. When you seek Him first in your operations, offers, and outreach, He'll provide everything else you need — clients, clarity, confidence, and capacity.

Strategy Tip

Let purpose lead your pricing and offerings. Don't just create what sells — create what serves. Revenue flows when your mission is clear and your heart is aligned.

Practical Tip

- Write a **mission-driven elevator pitch** that explains why your business exists — not just what you sell.
- Practice sharing it with confidence and conviction.
- Update your website and social media bios to clearly reflect your purpose and who you serve.

Purpose Notes: Purpose Check-In

Revisit your offers, pricing, and promotions. Are they aligned with your God-given assignment — or just designed to bring in fast cash?

Cut anything that doesn't serve your mission or your audience. What honors God will multiply.

Prayer

Lord, help me never place profit above purpose. Keep my heart aligned with Your Kingdom purpose. Remind me that provision is a result of obedience, not striving.

Use my business as a vessel for Your influence and truth. Let everything I build reflect Your heart and glorify Your name. In Jesus' name, amen.

DAY 4

Invest in Wisdom

Scripture

> "Wisdom is the principal thing; therefore get wisdom.
> And in all your getting, get understanding."
>
> — Proverbs 4:7 (NKJV)

Devotion

Anointing may open the door, but **wisdom builds the house.** You are gifted, called, and favored — but in order to steward the vision well, you need more than passion. You need **strategy, structure,** and **sound instruction.**

Too often, entrepreneurs pray for growth but resist the very tools and guidance that sustain it. God's Word doesn't suggest wisdom — it commands us to *get* it. That means you must **pursue it intentionally**, with a teachable spirit and a willingness to be stretched.

Even Jesus "grew in wisdom" (Luke 2:52). If our Savior saw the value in growing intellectually and spiritually, how much more should we?

Wisdom may come through:

- A mentor or coach
- A course or certification
- A book or life experience

And yes — wisdom comes with a cost. It might be time, pride, or money. But what you invest in wisdom, you'll reap in results and legacy.

Don't equate struggling with being spiritual. Hosea 4:6 says, *"My people are destroyed for lack of knowledge."* God honors both your **faith** and your **follow-through**. Seek His guidance — and back it up with action.

Strategy Tip

Identify the **top 3 areas** in your business where you feel stuck or unsure.

Pray over each one.

Then ask God to guide you to the right **resource, mentor, or system** to address them this quarter.

Practical Tip

Set aside **5–10% of your monthly business income** specifically for professional growth—books, coaching, training, or automation tools.

Think of it as **tithing to your development**. It's not an expense—it's a seed.

Purpose Notes: Growth Requires Guidance

You don't have to figure it all out alone.

Wisdom is an investment, not a luxury.

Get the help, training, and tools you need to operate with excellence. God can't bless what you won't build with care.

Prayer

Lord, I thank You for the anointing on my life, but I also ask for the wisdom to manage what You've placed in my hands. Lead me to the right resources, mentors, and systems that align with Your will. Make me teachable, discerning, and faithful with the vision You've given me. Multiply the seeds of wisdom I sow. In Jesus' name, amen.

Faith to Build

DAY 5

Trusting God's Timing

Scripture

> *"To everything there is a season, a time for every purpose under heaven."*
> — Ecclesiastes 3:1 (NKJV)

Devotion

In Kingdom business, **timing is everything**. You can have the right idea, the right strategy, and even the right anointing — but if it's not God's appointed time, the door won't open.

That doesn't mean God has forgotten you. It means He's forming you.

Waiting isn't wasted time — it's **preparation**. In the stillness, God is sharpening your character, strengthening your faith, and aligning your purpose with His perfect plan. Just as a seed must endure seasons before harvest, your business must also walk through **development before elevation.**

Sometimes, the very thing you're praying for would overwhelm you if it came too soon. **Divine delays are not denials — they are protection.**

There is **wisdom in slow growth**, and **strength in stillness**. When God says it's your season, no one can stop the acceleration He releases.

Strategy Tip

Design a 12-month business roadmap, but keep it flexible.

Ask yourself:

- Are my timelines based on pressure or purpose?
- Am I pushing a deadline that God hasn't assigned?
- Surrender your schedule to Him and trust His divine detours.

Practical Tip

Before launching anything new — product, service, or strategy — run a **3-part timing check:**

1. Spiritual Confirmation (Have you prayed and received peace?)
2. Market Validation (Do you have data or feedback to support the need?)
3. Operational Readiness (Do you have the systems, tools, and support in place?)

Launch with order, not impulse.

Purpose Notes: You're Right on Kingdom Time

What God is doing in you behind the scenes is just as valuable as what He'll do through you publicly.

Trust that the wait is producing something weighty.

So don't panic. You're not late — you're right on Kingdom time.

Favor has a schedule — and when it's time, acceleration will come effortlessly.

Prayer

God, help me to rest in Your timing. I release my need to control the calendar. Align my pace with Your purpose. I trust that what You are preparing for me — and in me — is worth the wait. Let me not be moved by pressure, but anchored in Your peace. In Jesus' name, amen.

Faith to Build

DAY 6

Provision for the Vision

Scripture

> "But my God shall supply all your need
> according to his riches in glory by Christ Jesus."
>
> — Philippians 4:19

Devotion

God funds what He ordains. He is not only the **Vision-Giver** — He is the **Provider**. If He called you to build it, He has already prepared the provision for it.

Stop stressing over what's lacking and start standing on what He promised. **Lack may be real**, but **it is not final**. You are not sustained by clients, contracts, or sales — you are sustained by the **Source**.

Even in financial wilderness seasons, **God rains down provision in unexpected ways.** His supply often comes in just enough to stretch your faith, sharpen your stewardship, and keep you dependent on Him.

Don't hustle from fear — build from trust.

Jehovah Jireh isn't moved by the market or economy. His provision flows from His promise — not your performance.

Strategy Tip

Be a steward of what you already have. Start here:

- Track your income and expenses weekly to notice patterns of God's provision
- Identify waste or inefficiency, and make faith-based adjustments
- Begin building an emergency fund — even if it's just $10/week

Stewardship invites more supply.

Practical Tip

Set up **automatic transfers** from each business income deposit:

- 10% to a **tithe account**
- 20–30% to an **emergency or tax savings account**
- The remainder into **operating expenses**

Even small seeds create harvests when God is your multiplier.

Purpose Notes: God Finances Purpose

If God gave the vision, He already lined up the resources, relationships, and revenue to fulfill it.

Provision is not always excess — it's often just enough to test your faith and teach you to trust.

God is not looking for panic — He's looking for stewardship.

You build in faith. He funds in full.

Prayer

Lord, thank You for being my Provider. Help me trust You even when the numbers don't add up. Jehovah Jireh, I trust You for every resource I need — capital, clients, and divine connections. You are my Source. I will not operate from fear or scarcity, but from Your supernatural supply. Amen.

Faith to Build

DAY 7

The Cost of Obedience

Scripture

> *"For which of you, intending to build a tower, sitteth not down first, and counteth the cost, whether he have sufficient to finish it?"*
>
> — Luke 14:28

Devotion

Obedience always costs something — but it costs far less than disobedience.

When God gives you an instruction, it often stretches you. You may be called to walk away from familiar routines, comfortable partnerships, or short-term profits. But every step of obedience you take is an investment into supernatural reward.

Your "yes" to God is more powerful than any business plan.

It's not always glamorous, and it's rarely convenient. But obedience invites God to build with you — and He never under-delivers.

Your obedience will cost you something — but it will birth everything.

Strategy Tip

Take time this week to **count the cost:**

- What is God asking you to release, start, or shift in your business?
- What systems, people, or habits are no longer aligned with your calling?

Make a **"Sacrifice & Surrender" list** and pray through it daily. Let this be your recommitment moment.

Practical Tip

Choose **one obedience-based action** you've been delaying — whether it's registering your business, hiring help, raising your prices, or walking away from a misaligned opportunity. Take a small step toward it **within the next 48 hours.**

Progress begins where obedience meets action.

Purpose Notes: Obedience Unlocks Blessing

Obedience often means discomfort — but it unlocks God's blessing.

Every "cost" is an investment in His greater plan.

Don't shrink from sacrifice — embrace it as your pathway to breakthrough.

Prayer

Father, give me the courage to obey even when it costs. Help me to count the cost with faith, not fear. I trust that what You're building through me is worth every sacrifice. I surrender my will for Yours. In Jesus' name, amen.

DAY 8

Building Generational Wealth

Scripture

> "A good man leaves an inheritance to his children's children..."
> — Proverbs 13:22 (NKJV)

Devotion

This business is not just for today — it's for tomorrow and beyond. You're not simply making money; you're laying a foundation that will echo through generations. You are the **cycle-breaker**, the pioneer called to shift the narrative.

Building generational wealth isn't only financial — it's spiritual, emotional, and intellectual. You are passing down faith, values, systems, and strategies that will empower your children's children to rise higher.

This is legacy work. Don't just chase income — build **impact**. Let your business reflect eternity. Don't take this lightly — take it prayerfully.

Strategy Tip

Don't just build income — build systems that can outlive you. Think **three generations ahead**. Your daily actions shape the family narrative and influence the legacy your descendants will inherit.

Practical Tip

Set up a custodial Roth IRA or a family trust as a long-term wealth vehicle.

Start your **Legacy Binder** — include important documents and notes like:

- Standard Operating Procedures (SOPs)
- Your will and estate planning details, including trusts and **succession plans**
- Passwords and access information
- Insurance policies, including **life insurance**
- Education savings plans, such as **529 plans** for your children
- Your **operating agreement** to clarify business ownership and roles

Organizing these now ensures your legacy is protected, transferable, and sustainable.

Purpose Notes: Legacy Is More Than Money

Generational wealth is faith passed down, wisdom shared, and systems created.

Your business is a platform for eternal impact — building not just for now, but for always.

Prayer

Lord, help me build something that outlives me. May my business, my values, and my wealth serve generations I may never see. Let my legacy bring You glory and lead my family into freedom. In Jesus' name, amen.

DAY 9

Resting While Building

Scripture

> *"My presence will go with you, and I will give you rest."*
> — Exodus 33:14

Devotion

Hustle culture is not holy. Kingdom entrepreneurs aren't called to burn out for success — we're called to build from a place of **rest, faith, and trust.**

God blesses rest. When you pause to rest in Him, He moves on your behalf. Rest isn't just physical — it's spiritual alignment. It declares: *"God is my Source, not my schedule."*

Rest is also a weapon. It fights anxiety. It silences self-reliance. It renews your vision. God created the Sabbath not just as a commandment, but as a gift — because when you rest, you're reminded that He's already working.

Rest is obedience. Rest is trust. Rest is strategy.

Strategy Tip

Schedule your **weekly Sabbath.**

- Pick one day or afternoon each week to unplug
- Mark it in your planner like any other important meeting
- Use that time to worship, reflect, and restore

Protect your peace like it's your greatest asset — because it is.

Practical Tip

Set **digital boundaries:**

- Turn off business notifications after a set hour each day
- Use automation tools (e.g., HoneyBook, Dubsado, social schedulers) to reduce manual work.
- Avoid working on Sundays (or your designated Sabbath) unless absolutely necessary

You are most productive when you're most **rested.**

Purpose Notes: Rest Is a Kingdom Strategy

Rest is not laziness — it's a divine appointment.

When you rest, you align with God's rhythm and release control.

Trust that His presence is your greatest source of strength.

Prayer

Jesus, teach me to rest in You. Help me operate from peace, not pressure. Remind me daily that my provision is not in my performance, but in Your promise. I choose to rest and trust that You're working even when I'm not. Amen.

Faith to Build

DAY 10

Excellence Reflects the Kingdom

Scripture

> *"Then this Daniel became distinguished above all the other presidents and satraps because an excellent spirit was in him..."*
> — Daniel 6:3

Devotion

Excellence isn't perfection — it's consistency, integrity, and doing all things as unto God. Your excellence sets you apart and reflects the King you serve. In a world where shortcuts are celebrated, choosing excellence is a form of worship.

Excellence is how you preach without speaking.

It shows up in your service, your emails, your client interactions, and your deliverables. It shows the world that you don't just represent a business — you represent the Kingdom.

God doesn't expect flawlessness, but He does expect faithfulness. Doing the small things with great care speaks volumes about your character and your calling. Don't do it for applause — **do it for Him.**

Strategy Tip

- **Collect reviews and testimonials** at the end of every project or monthly cycle
- Use this feedback to identify where you can raise the bar
- **Audit one area** of your business this week — branding, client experience, financial records, communication — and ask, *"Does this reflect the excellence of God?"*

Practical Tip

Create an **Excellence Checklist** for your business operations. Review things like:

- Response time to emails or inquiries
- Professionalism of contracts and proposals
- Use client onboarding workflows and email templates to elevate your service experience.
- Team communication and accountability

Set a reminder to review this checklist monthly or quarterly.

Purpose Notes: Excellence is Kingdom Impact

Excellence is not about perfection, but about honoring God in all you do.

Your work becomes a testimony to His glory.

Prayer

Lord, let excellence be my standard — not for applause, but as a reflection of Your Kingdom. Help me steward every part of my business with integrity, humility, and consistency. May my work glorify You in the seen and unseen. In Jesus' name, amen.

DAY 11

The Right Structure

Scripture

> *"Let all things be done decently and in order."*
> — 1 Corinthians 14:40 (KJV)

Devotion

Heaven honors order. Just as the temple was built with intentional structure, your business must also be established on **legal, financial, and operational integrity**. The right business structure isn't just paperwork — it's **spiritual stewardship**.

Structure determines sustainability. Without the right foundation, success can become a burden instead of a blessing. When your business is structured properly, you create space for **clarity, protection, and scalability**. It shows God — and others — that you are serious about what you're building.

Don't skip the legalities. Don't avoid the financial systems. Whether you're building from scratch or rebuilding from experience, do it with wisdom and intentionality.

Strategy Tip

Book a session with a **tax advisor, accountant, or business attorney** to:

- Choose the right entity (LLC, S-Corp, Corporation)
- Understand your tax obligations
- Create a compliance checklist for licenses, filings, and renewals

The right structure is a gateway to favor, funding, and freedom.

Practical Tip

Open a **dedicated business bank account** and:

- Separate personal and business finances
- Track income, expenses, and profit monthly using tools like QuickBooks, Wave, or Excel
- Build a financial habit of reconciliation and monthly review

Clean records protect your vision and prepare you for growth, audits, grants, and investments.

Purpose Notes: Order Invites Increase

Excellence starts with structure.

God won't bless a mess — He blesses what is in order.

Structure is not legalism. It's leadership.

Prayer

God, show me how to structure my business with excellence. Let me not move in haste but in wisdom and order. Help me build something that honors You and is prepared for increase. In Jesus' name, amen.

Faith to Build

DAY 12

Building with Integrity

Scripture

> "The integrity of the upright will guide them,
> but the crookedness of the treacherous destroys them."
>
> — Proverbs 11:3 (ESV)

Devotion

Integrity is more than being honest — it's **consistency in character**, especially when no one is watching. It's doing the right thing when it's inconvenient, costly, or unseen.

In the world of entrepreneurship, shortcuts and "gray areas" often seem tempting — especially when cash flow is tight or opportunity knocks in disguise. But the Kingdom way is the **honest way** — and God honors what is built on **truth**.

Your **name** is more valuable than any sale. Your **word** is a seed. Your **integrity** is spiritual currency — it opens doors that hustle alone can't. While others chase quick wins, you're building something that will last.

God will not bless what compromises His principles. He cannot anoint deception. But a business founded on integrity becomes a **vessel of trust**, a light in dark systems, and a legacy-builder for generations.

Let your "yes" be yes and your "no" be no — not just with clients, but with God. Behind every invoice, contract, and conversation, ask:

Can this stand before God?

Let integrity guide your pricing, policies, partnerships, and public image. Don't just build to be seen — **build to be remembered in Heaven.**

Strategy Tip

Do a **personal and business audit** this week:

- Are your prices fair and reflective of the value you provide?
- Are you accurately reporting income and expenses?
- Do your systems and client interactions reflect honesty and clarity?

Make necessary changes and pray over them. Ask God to bless clean hands and pure motives.

Practical Tip

Always use **contracts**, even with friends or family. Put everything in writing:

- Services
- Scope
- Timelines
- Payment terms

This protects your business, your relationships, and your reputation — and honors your commitment to transparency.

Purpose Notes: Integrity Is the Foundation of Influence

Your gift may open the door, but integrity is what keeps you in the room.

Build slow if you must, but build honest. That's where God releases favor.

Prayer

Lord, make me a person of integrity in every area of my life and business. Help me build with honesty, steward relationships with truth, and reflect Your character even when no one is watching. Let my business be a light that brings You glory and sets a new standard in the marketplace. Amen.

Faith to Build

DAY 13

When to Pivot or Persevere

Scripture

> *"And let us not be weary in well doing:
> for in due season we shall reap, if we faint not."*
>
> — Galatians 6:9 (KJV)

Devotion

One of the hardest decisions in business is knowing whether to pivot or persevere. Sometimes God is telling you to wait — and other times, He's telling you to move. Discernment is key.

Just because it's hard doesn't mean it's time to quit. But just because you've been doing it for a long time doesn't mean it's still aligned. Kingdom entrepreneurs must be both **faithful and flexible** — anchored in the vision, but open to divine redirection.

Waiting is not wasting when you're aligned with God's will. But ignoring His prompting out of fear or pride can become disobedience. Ask: Is God calling me to press through, or is He calling me to shift course?

Remember, your faithfulness is never wasted — but wisdom will teach you where to pour that faith.

Strategy Tip

Set aside time this week to review what's not working in your business. Ask:

- Is this issue a test of endurance or a sign to shift?
- Am I holding on out of faith—or fear of change?
- What would obedience look like in this area?

Talk with a mentor, review your data, and bring the question to God in prayer.

Practical Tip

Identify 1–2 areas in your business that feel stagnant or frustrating.

- Evaluate your offers, marketing, partnerships, or time investment.
- Be honest: What needs to be improved, paused, or reimagined?

Small pivots can lead to major breakthroughs when God is guiding the shift.

Purpose Notes: Know the Difference

There's a difference between being persistent and being stuck.

Sometimes faith looks like staying the course. Other times, it looks like starting over — with God's permission.

Prayer

Lord, give me discernment to know when to pivot and when to persevere. Help me to move with You — not ahead of You or behind You. Align my heart with Your direction, and give me peace whether I'm called to remain or release. In Jesus' name, amen.

Faith to Build

DAY 14

Attracting the Right Clients

Scripture

> "A man's gift maketh room for him, and bringeth him before great men."
> — Proverbs 18:16 (KJV)

Devotion

You're not for everyone — and that's okay. Your business isn't meant to appeal to the masses; it's designed to serve those God has **divinely assigned** to you.

When you operate boldly in your gift, the right clients — those who value your expertise, align with your mission, and honor your pricing — will be drawn to you. You don't need to **strive, chase, or compromise**. Your anointing attracts. Your authenticity is magnetic.

God never calls you to fit in — He calls you to **stand out**. When your brand is rooted in your God-given identity, it becomes a beacon for your ideal audience. So stop chasing people who were never meant to walk with you. Focus on serving from a place of **clarity, confidence, and calling** — and trust God to send divine connections.

Strategy Tip

Create a **Dream Client Profile** that includes:

- Age and stage of life or business
- Core values and personality traits
- Pain points you solve
- Budget comfort level
- Preferred communication style
- Buying behavior

Use this profile to sharpen your message and align your marketing with who you're truly meant to serve.

Practical Tip

Audit your **website, social media, and marketing materials:**

- Do they reflect who you serve and how you serve them?
- Is your messaging clear, confident, and Christ-centered?

Update your content to speak directly to your dream client's language, needs, and desires.

Purpose Notes: Your Gift Is the Magnet

You don't need to beg for business.

Stand in your calling. Refine your message. Trust the God who gave you the gift to also bring the audience.

Prayer

Father, align me with those I'm called to serve. Let my business attract clients who are honorable, ready, and aligned with the purpose You've placed on my life. May my gift make room and my brand reflect Your excellence. In Jesus' name, amen.

Faith to Build

DAY 15

Pricing with Confidence

Scripture

> *"...the worker deserves his wages."*
> — Luke 10:7 (NIV)

Devotion

There is nothing humble about undercharging. As a Kingdom entrepreneur, your pricing should reflect your **value**, not your **insecurities**. God is not glorified when you shrink to please people or avoid rejection.

You've been equipped, trained, and anointed to serve with excellence — and excellence has a price. Jesus taught that the laborer is worthy of their wages. That includes you. When you discount your worth out of fear, you dishonor the value of the assignment God has given you.

Your price should reflect your preparation, your impact, and your obedience — not fear, guilt, or comparison. Pricing with confidence is an act of stewardship. It shows that you honor what God has placed in your hands and trust Him to send the right clients who see and respect your value.

Strategy Tip

If fear, people-pleasing, or comparison have shaped your pricing — pause.

Go back to the value you bring. Consider your results, your growth, your commitment.

Let **value, clarity, and confidence** set your price, not pressure.

Practical Tip

Review your current pricing.

Are you charging based on fear or faith?

Do your rates reflect your expertise — or insecurity?

- Adjust where needed.
- Document your client results or testimonials.
- Use that data to validate your value.

Purpose Notes: Confidence Is Stewardship

You are not charging for your salvation — you're charging for your service.

Your gifts make room for you, and the right clients will honor what you carry.

Pricing with confidence is part of doing business God's way.

Prayer

Lord, help me price with boldness and worth. Remove the fear that causes me to shrink or second-guess what You've called me to do. Help me operate in excellence and integrity — and trust You to send the clients assigned to my voice. In Jesus' name, amen.

Faith to Build

DAY 16

Overcoming Comparison

Scripture

> "Each one should test their own actions. Then they can take pride in themselves alone, without comparing themselves to someone else."
>
> — Galatians 6:4 (NIV)

Devotion

Comparison is the enemy of contentment. In business, it's easy to glance sideways at what others are building and start doubting your pace, process, or potential. But what God is doing in your life is **sacred, unique, and right on schedule.**

Your anointing cannot be copied. Your calling won't look like anyone else's. Just like seeds planted in different seasons bloom at different times, so will your harvest — **when it's time.**

Instead of comparing, **celebrate others.** *Their win is proof that God is moving. Let their success build your faith, not feed your insecurity. Then turn your eyes back to your own field and keep watering it. You are not behind — you are being* **built.**

Strategy Tip

Audit your digital environment this week:

- *Unfollow or mute accounts that stir comparison or self-doubt*
- *Follow content that builds your **faith, clarity, and confidence***
- *Set time limits on social media to protect your focus and emotional well-being*

Practical Tip

*Start a **Progress Journal**:*

- *Each week, write down 3 wins — big or small*
- *Track what you're learning, implementing, and improving*
- *Revisit these entries to remind yourself how far you've come and how faithful God has been*

This builds gratitude and quiets the noise of comparison.

Purpose Notes: Comparison Cancels Clarity

God's plan for you is custom — not copy and paste.

Stay in your lane. Water your own garden. Trust His timing.

Prayer

God, help me to fix my eyes on You and the path You've set before me. Silence the voice of comparison and fill me with confidence in what You've called me to do. Remind me daily that my timeline is ordained by Heaven. In Jesus' name, amen.

DAY 17

Networking with Kingdom Purpose

Scripture

> *"Two are better than one, because they have a good return for their labor."*
> — Ecclesiastes 4:9 (NIV)

Devotion

God did not call you to build in isolation. Your assignment is too weighty to carry alone. **Kingdom networking** is not about popularity — it's about **purposeful alignment.**

When God sends the right people, He's sending wisdom, support, strategy — and sometimes, your next opportunity. The right relationships accelerate destiny. The wrong ones distract it.

Every divine connection is a seed. Be intentional about who you collaborate with, and **prayerful about who you allow to speak into your vision**. Not every open door is ordained, and not every platform is for you.

Ask the Holy Spirit to guide your connections, protect your circle, and position you to **both give and receive value.**

Strategy Tip

Identify **1–2 people** this month within your industry or faith circle whom you feel led to connect with.

- Reach out with intention
- Set up a connection call or coffee chat
- Be clear about your purpose and open to mutual growth

Bonus: Meals and meetings with clear business intent are considered tax-deductible business expenses. Track them accordingly.

Practical Tip

Create a **Networking Tracker Spreadsheet:**

- Include names, where you met, what you discussed, and follow-up action items
- Set reminders to stay in touch
- Use it to cultivate real relationships — not just contacts

Purpose Notes: Purpose Over Popularity

It's not about how many people you know — it's about how many God-ordained connections you're nurturing.

Protect your energy. Steward your relationships. Pray before you partner.

Prayer

Lord, connect me with people who sharpen me, strengthen me, and align with Your purpose for my life and business. Help me discern divine connections and be a blessing in return. In Jesus' name, amen.

DAY 18

Spirit-Led Branding

Scripture

> *"You are the light of the world. A town built on a hill cannot be hidden."*
> — Matthew 5:14 (NIV)

Devotion

You were never meant to blend in — you were born to stand out. As a Kingdom entrepreneur, your brand is more than colors, fonts, or a catchy slogan. **Your brand is the expression of your divine assignment.** It reflects your values, your voice, and the glory of the God you serve.

When your brand is Spirit-led, it doesn't just attract — it **transforms**. Clients won't just see your business — they'll encounter clarity, authenticity, and light. That's why you must resist the temptation to copy someone else's identity. Their oil won't work for your assignment.

You are graced for a specific audience. Your tone — whether nurturing, bold, prophetic, or professional — must reflect the anointing on your life. Branding led by the Holy Spirit will always speak louder than trends.

When your brand is built with clarity, purpose, and integrity, it becomes a tool for impact, influence, and Kingdom expansion.

Strategy Tip

Take time today to clarify these four pillars:

- What is my brand's message?
- What problems do I solve?
- Who am I called to serve?
- How do I want people to feel when they engage with my brand?

Then align your **visuals, tone, and content** with that identity. Let your branding reflect both **your excellence and your anointing.**

Practical Tip

Create a simple **Brand Identity Board** using tools like Canva or Pinterest. Include:

- Brand colors and fonts
- Mission statement and tagline
- Visual inspiration and sample language
- Client testimonials that reflect your impact

Let this board keep you focused and consistent as you grow.

Purpose Notes: Spirit Over Strategy

Strategy matters — but when it's led by the Spirit, your brand becomes a vessel for impact, authenticity, and favor.

You're not building for popularity. You're building to be seen for His glory.

Prayer

Holy Spirit, guide my brand. Let every element reflect Your wisdom, creativity, and truth. Remove the desire to compete or copy. I trust that what You've placed in me is enough. Let my business be a light on a hill — visible, valuable, and full of Your glory. In Jesus' name, amen.

FAITH TO BUILD

DAY 19

Multiplication & Expansion

Scripture

> *"Be fruitful and multiply; fill the earth and subdue it."*
> — Genesis 1:28 (NKJV)

Devotion

You were not created to stay small. **Expansion is your portion.** God's very first command wasn't just to exist — it was to grow, to take territory, and to fill the earth with purpose.

As a Kingdom entrepreneur, you are anointed for multiplication. This isn't just about increasing revenue — it's about expanding your **impact, influence, and legacy.** Expansion doesn't mean chasing everything. It means multiplying what already carries God's favor.

Growth happens when you prepare for it. That means building systems, strengthening your structure, and trusting God's timing. Don't fear growth — **make room for it**. Stretch your mindset, build your infrastructure, and pray bold, strategic prayers. You are not called to blend in — you're called to take up space for the glory of God.

Strategy Tip

Identify **one system** in your business that you can automate or scale this month:

- Invoicing
- Email responses
- Appointment scheduling
- Client onboarding

Freeing up your time in these areas creates space for vision, leadership, and legacy-level work.

Practical Tip

Choose one tool to support your next level of growth. Consider:

- **HoneyBook** – client management
- **QuickBooks** – financial tracking
- **Calendly** – scheduling
- **ConvertKit** – email automation

These tools are not only helpful — they're considered **tax-deductible business expenses**. Document them properly and consult your tax advisor for optimal deductions.

Purpose Notes: Multiply with Intention

Growth without structure leads to chaos.

Faith + Strategy + Stewardship = Sustainable Expansion

Prayer

Lord, I thank You that I am not called to remain small. Stretch my capacity and mindset to embrace growth. Give me divine clarity, bold strategy, and supernatural courage to step into multiplication. I receive expansion as my portion, and I will steward it faithfully. In Jesus' name, amen.

Faith to Build

DAY 20

Credit as Kingdom Capital

Scripture

> *"Whoever can be trusted with very little can also be trusted with much..."*

— Luke 16:10

Devotion

As Kingdom entrepreneurs, we are called to steward every area of our lives — including our financial reputation — with purpose and integrity. Credit is not just a personal tool; it is Kingdom capital. When managed wisely, it becomes a vehicle for expansion, access, and favor in both business and personal endeavors.

For business owners, good credit is critical. It can determine your ability to secure funding, lease commercial space, purchase equipment, or qualify for government contracts. It is often the first measure of your trustworthiness and financial stewardship in the eyes of lenders and investors. Without it, many doors remain closed — no matter how great your vision is.

When you treat credit as a form of capital, you begin to manage it with Kingdom strategy — not fear. Just as a builder wouldn't begin a project without materials, you should not ignore the financial tools God has placed at your disposal. Regularly checking your credit, understanding your score, and correcting errors are simple yet powerful ways to walk in wisdom and open doors for Kingdom impact.

Strategy Tip

Business and personal credit both matter. Establish and build your business credit by opening a business bank account, applying for a D-U-N-S number, and using vendor credit lines. Maintain good standing with payments and keep utilization low.

Practical Tip

Review both your personal and business credit reports annually. Use AnnualCreditReport.com for personal credit, and Nav.com or Dun & Bradstreet for business credit tracking. Dispute errors quickly and keep business expenses separate from personal finances.

Purpose Note

Strong credit reflects your integrity and preparation. As a Kingdom entrepreneur, it positions you for increase, influence, and opportunities that align with God's assignment for your life and business.

Reflection Questions

- How have I used or misused credit in the past?
- What steps can I take now to establish or improve my business credit?
- Am I honoring God in how I handle credit as part of my financial stewardship?

Prayer

Lord, thank You for giving me access to resources that support my vision. Help me to manage both personal and business credit with discipline and integrity. Give me wisdom to build a strong financial foundation that reflects Your character and opens doors for Kingdom opportunities. I trust You to guide me in every financial decision. In Jesus' name, Amen.

DAY 21

Hiring with Discernment

Scripture

> "But select capable men from all the people — men who fear God, trustworthy men who hate dishonest gain — and appoint them as officials over thousands, hundreds, fifties and tens."

— Exodus 18:21 (NKJV)

Devotion

Your business is only as strong as the team behind it. But not every helper is divinely sent. Hiring without discernment can lead to distraction, compromise, and burnout. God's guidance is essential when choosing those who will stand with you.

Seek covenant workers — people who not only have the skills you need but also embrace your mission, reflect your values, and walk in integrity. These are partners in purpose, not just employees.

Hiring with spiritual wisdom brings unity, multiplies your impact, and protects your vision. Pray fervently for God's hand in your hiring decisions and trust His timing.

Strategy Tip

Develop a **Hiring Checklist** that includes:

- Spiritual Alignment: Do they share your faith values or respect your Kingdom vision?
- Skill Set: Do they possess the expertise and experience required?
- Integrity: Are they trustworthy and honest?

Long-term Potential: Can they grow with your business and contribute to your legacy?

Use this checklist in interviews and reference checks.

Practical Tip

Before hiring, clearly define the role, responsibilities, and expectations in writing. Include how the position supports your mission and culture. This clarity helps attract candidates who resonate deeply with your vision.

Purpose Notes: Hiring Help Legally & Lovingly

- Start with a virtual assistant or contractor to ease workload without heavy commitments.
- Use clear onboarding processes and written contracts to protect your business.
- Remember: Hiring expenses, onboarding, and training can be tax-deductible business expenses.
- Delegate tasks that free your time to focus on high-impact areas of your business.
- Pray for wisdom and discernment to build a trustworthy and aligned team.

Prayer

Lord, I ask for Your divine guidance in building my team. Bring to me covenant workers who are skilled, trustworthy, and aligned with Your purpose for my business. Let every hire strengthen my vision and glorify You. In Jesus' name, amen.

Faith to Build

DAY 22

Stewarding Wealth Wisely

Scripture

> *"The wise store up choice food and olive oil, but fools gulp theirs down."*
> — Proverbs 21:20 (NIV)

Devotion

Money isn't evil — it's a tool. What matters is how you manage it. As a Kingdom entrepreneur, your finances are a sacred trust. God has entrusted you with resources to manage, multiply, and release into His purposes.

Stewardship requires discipline, vision, and wisdom. It means planning beyond today, building reserves, and giving generously. When you wisely allocate your income, you not only secure your business's future but also open doors to bless others.

Don't let money control you — control your money with Kingdom principles. Be the business owner who builds, budgets, and multiplies what God gives.

Strategy Tip

Practice the **10-10-80 rule:**

- **10% Tithe:** Honor God first
- **10% Save:** Build an emergency fund and savings for growth
- **80% Expenses:** Operational costs and reinvestment

Track your income and expenses weekly to stay accountable and adjust as needed.

Practical Tip

Open separate accounts for:

- Tithes/Offerings
- Savings/Emergency Fund
- Operating Expenses

Automate transfers on payday to reinforce discipline and peace of mind.

Purpose Notes: Business & Tax Wealth Tips

- Keep detailed records of all business income and expenses for tax accuracy and maximized deductions.
- Deduct ordinary and necessary business expenses such as office supplies, software, utilities, and professional fees.
- Build an emergency fund equivalent to 3–6 months of operating expenses to protect your business.
- Consult a tax professional to leverage retirement accounts like SEP IRAs or Solo 401(k)s for tax-advantaged savings.
- Regularly review and adjust your budget as your business grows to maintain financial health.

Prayer

Lord, help me become a wise steward of the resources You've given me. Teach me discipline in managing my finances and generosity in giving. Let every dollar be a seed for growth, provision, and blessing. I commit my business and finances to Your glory. In Jesus' name, amen.

Faith to Build

DAY 23

Protecting the Vision

Scripture

> *"No weapon formed against you shall prosper,*
> *and every tongue which rises against you in judgment You shall condemn."*
>
> — Isaiah 54:17 (NKJV)

Devotion

Every **God-given vision** will face resistance. Whether it's spiritual warfare, legal battles, copycats, or distractions — if it's from God, it will be tested. But take heart: **what God ordains, He protects.**

Your vision is sacred. It's not just an idea — it's an assignment. That means it must be guarded in both **prayer and practice.** You are not just building for profit; you're building for purpose. And purpose must be protected.

As a Kingdom entrepreneur, you need both **spiritual armor** and **natural wisdom**. Stay prayerful and discerning, but also strategic and covered. Don't share everything prematurely. Don't leave what God gave you exposed.

Like Nehemiah, who built with a sword in one hand and a tool in the other, you must build with **prayer in one hand and protection in the other.**

Strategy Tip

Expect opposition. Every Kingdom assignment draws attention in the spiritual and natural realms.

- Stay armored in **prayer**
- Stay focused on your **assignment**
- Stay wise in your **execution**

Practical Tip

Protect your business assets:

- Use **NDAs** when sharing proprietary ideas or content
- File **copyrights/trademarks** for your brand materials
- Secure digital files and system access
- Include clear refund, cancellation, and privacy policies in all client agreements and platforms
- **Consult a trusted business attorney whenever possible** to ensure your protections are legally sound

Business Protection Checklist

Use this checklist to guard your business legally and spiritually:

- Signed contracts for every client/project
- Trademark or copyright filings for brand name, logo, and content
- Clear refund, cancellation, and privacy policies in writing
- A consistent prayer routine for daily or weekly business covering

Protection is part of stewardship. Don't just launch — cover it.

Purpose Notes: Guard What God Gave You

Not everything God shows you is meant to be shared publicly.

Protect the vision spiritually through prayer, and legally through systems.

Vision leaks where there is no covering.

Guard it until God says go.

Prayer

Lord, thank You for entrusting me with this vision. Teach me to protect it with wisdom, discernment, and obedience. I cover my business, ideas, and strategies in prayer. Keep me focused and alert. Help me build with excellence and guard what You've given me from both spiritual attack and natural misuse. In Jesus' name, amen.

Faith to Build

DAY 24

Becoming a Blessing

Scripture

> *"...I will bless you... and you will be a blessing."*
> — Genesis 12:2 (NIV)

Devotion

Your business is not just a means of provision — it's a vessel for generosity. You were never meant to be a reservoir. You are a river. God blesses us not just to increase our lives, but to impact the lives of others.

When you bless others, you align with the very heart of God. A Kingdom business doesn't hoard — it helps. It feeds vision, funds ministries, empowers families, and creates opportunities for those who've been overlooked.

Be intentional about being a blessing. It doesn't always have to be financial. Your wisdom, your time, your platform, and your voice are powerful gifts.

You are the answer to someone's prayer. Let your business reflect Heaven's compassion.

Strategy Tip

This quarter, choose one mission or organization — a church, youth program, single-parent family, or Kingdom initiative — to sow into.

Set a giving goal (financial, time, or services). Track the impact and ask God how to grow that seed.

Practical Tip

Add a **"Give Back"** line to your business budget or pricing model. For example:

- "5% of every service supports _____."
- Or offer a quarterly free workshop or mentorship spot.

This aligns your brand with mission and draws clients who value purpose-driven impact.

Purpose Notes: Business & Tax Tips for Giving

- Charitable contributions made through your business can be tax-deductible if properly documented—consult your accountant for specifics.
- Track all donations, volunteer hours, and in-kind gifts to maximize tax benefits and impact reporting.
- Consider setting up a formal giving fund within your business to streamline generosity and budgeting.
- Use giving as a marketing differentiator by sharing stories of impact to attract like-minded clients.
- Generosity opens doors for divine favor and business opportunities beyond measure.

Prayer

Father, make me a generous steward. Help me bless others with my time, resources, and service. Use my business to fund freedom, spark hope, and heal hearts. Let my obedience overflow into others' breakthroughs. In Jesus' name, amen.

DAY 25

Walking in Favor

Scripture

> *"Surely, Lord, you bless the righteous;*
> *you surround them with your favor as with a shield."*
>
> — Psalm 5:12 (NIV)

Devotion

Favor is not earned — it's granted. It's the supernatural endorsement of Heaven on your assignment. Favor is what causes people to say yes when logic says no. It places your name in rooms you've never entered and aligns you with opportunities you didn't apply for.

You don't have to strive for what God has already prepared. Your job is obedience; His job is favor. When you walk uprightly, favor becomes your covering, your shield, and your testimony.

It's time to stop shrinking. Walk into that meeting, that pitch, that launch — knowing that favor is surrounding you like a force field. Walk into that meeting, that pitch, that launch — confident that favor is enveloping you like a protective shield.. You're not just showing up — you're being sent.

Strategy Tip

Write down 3 bold, faith-filled "stretch" opportunities for this year (e.g., a podcast feature, national speaking event, strategic partnership, corporate contract).

Pray over them daily. Declare favor over them. Prepare for them like they're already yours.

Practical Tip

Craft a professional **"Kingdom Resume"** or media kit — highlight your impact, services, testimonials, and God-glorifying mission. Keep it ready for divine opportunities.

Also, practice your elevator pitch — clear, bold, and anointed.

Purpose Notes: Business & Tax Tips

- Keep detailed records of your ministry and business activities to leverage opportunities for grants, sponsorships, or partnerships.
- Expenses related to promoting your business and mission (media kits, website, events) are tax-deductible.
- Use business cards, resumes, and promotional materials as investments in expanding your Kingdom influence and brand.
- Favor often comes through relationships — track and nurture key contacts professionally to build lasting networks.

Prayer

Father, I thank You that Your favor surrounds me. I declare doors are opening, timelines are accelerating, and hearts are softening because You've gone before me. Let Your favor speak where I cannot. Use me as a vessel for Kingdom influence and legacy. In Jesus' name, amen.

DAY 26

Time Management & Balance

Scripture

> *"To everything there is a season, a time for every purpose under heaven."*
> — Ecclesiastes 3:1

Devotion

As a Kingdom entrepreneur, your calendar is more than a schedule — it's a sacred trust. God doesn't call us to hustle without holiness or to grow a business while our faith and families suffer. True balance isn't about doing everything at once — it's about doing the right things in the right season.

There will be seasons of sowing and seasons of rest. Seasons of stretching and seasons of stillness. When you submit your time to God, He reveals what matters most. Busyness is not fruitfulness. Wisdom knows when to work and when to worship.

Honor your season. Don't compare your pace. Build from a place of grace.

Strategy Tip

Use time-blocking to bring order and peace to your week. Break your day into intentional blocks:

- Morning Power Hour – Prayer, devotion, planning
- CEO Time – Strategy, finances, vision-casting

- Client/Task Time – Focused work in your business
- Family Time – Fully present with loved ones
- Rest Block – Sabbath, self-care, sleep

Practical Tip

Pick one day each week (e.g., Sunday evening or Monday morning) to plan your schedule in advance. Color-code or label your time blocks:

- 🔵 Spiritual
- 🟢 Business
- 🟡 Family
- 🔴 Rest

Use a digital calendar or planner and protect those blocks like appointments with God.

Purpose Notes:
Quick Tips for Time Management & Balance

- **Plan Weekly:** Schedule your week in advance to reduce stress and increase focus.
- **Set Boundaries:** Turn off work notifications outside business hours to protect rest.
- **Prioritize Rest:** Sabbath isn't optional— it's a command and a blessing.
- **Use Tools:** Digital calendars (Google Calendar, Outlook) with color coding improve clarity.
- **Delegate:** Free your time by assigning tasks that don't require your unique skills.
- **Say No:** Protect your time by declining non-essential requests or commitments.

Prayer

Father, thank You for the gift of time. Teach me to steward my days with wisdom and grace. Help me create rhythms that honor my assignment, my family, and my health. Keep me from burnout and comparison. Remind me that fruitfulness flows from obedience, not overwhelm. In Jesus' name, amen.

Faith to Build

DAY 27

Financial Breakthroughs

Scripture

> *"But remember the Lord your God,
> for it is he who gives you the ability to produce wealth…"*
>
> — Deuteronomy 8:18

Devotion

God empowers you not only to receive provision but to generate lasting wealth. Financial breakthrough is a daily journey of faith, obedience, wisdom, and strategic action. The blueprint for your success is already in place — now it's time to step into it confidently.

Your wealth is a Kingdom responsibility, meant to fund your vision, bless others, and create a legacy that endures. Trust that you are anointed to build with purpose and authority.

Strategy Tip

Create a multi-stream income plan that fits your unique calling:

- Digital products (courses, e-books)
- Service offerings (coaching, speaking)
- Physical goods (merchandise, branded items)
- Real estate investments

Diversify to grow impact and income sustainably.

Practical Tip

Select one new income stream to develop this quarter. Plan the costs, platforms, and timeline. Pray over your plan and pursue it with focus and faith.

Purpose Notes: Financial Breakthrough Tips

1. **Track & Diversify:** Know your income sources and expand thoughtfully.
2. **Budget & Reinvest:** Allocate funds for growth and reinvest profits wisely.
3. **Build Emergency Savings:** Protect your business against unexpected setbacks.

Prayer

Lord, thank You for the ability to create wealth. Grant me wisdom and discipline to steward my resources well. Help me build a legacy that honors You and blesses others. In Jesus' name, amen.

DAY 28

Standing Out in the Market

Scripture

> *"Arise, shine, for your light has come,
> and the glory of the Lord rises upon you."*
>
> — Isaiah 60:1

Devotion

You weren't created to blend in — you were anointed to stand out. The world doesn't need another copy; it needs the authentic, Spirit-filled version of you. God uniquely designed your story, your voice, your solution, and your audience. When you embrace who you are in Him, your difference becomes your distinction.

The marketplace is full of noise, but Heaven is looking for light-bearers. You are a Kingdom ambassador, and your brand should reflect that. This is the hour to arise in clarity, confidence, and consecration. No more shrinking. No more hiding. Your anointing is your advantage.

You carry something no one else does, and it's time to unapologetically show up.

Strategy Tip

Craft a bold, Kingdom-centered "About Me" that reflects your story, values, mission, and the transformation you bring. Share your faith journey, your passion, and how your business glorifies God.

- Use phrases like: "I serve faith-driven entrepreneurs..." or "This business was born through prayer and purpose..."
- Make it personable, powerful, and faith-filled.

Practical Tip

Audit your website and social media bio. Are you clearly communicating:

- Who you serve?
- What you do differently?
- Why you're the solution to their problem?

Update your branding language with 2–3 core values and a strong call-to-action that reflects your God-given assignment.

Purpose Notes: Standing Out Tips

1. **Be Authentic:** Your true story and faith are your strongest brand assets.
2. **Communicate Clearly:** Make your mission and audience unmistakable.
3. **Consistent Messaging:** Align all platforms with your Kingdom values and voice.

Prayer

Father, I thank You that I am not hidden — I am chosen. Let me arise and shine with holy confidence. Make me visible to the people You've called me to serve. Let my light be distinct, my message clear, and my brand anointed. I will not shrink. I will stand. I will shine. In Jesus' name, amen.

Faith to Build

DAY 29

Leaving a Legacy

Scripture

> *"A good person leaves an inheritance for their children's children, but a sinner's wealth is stored up for the righteous."*
>
> — Proverbs 13:22

Devotion

Legacy isn't just about money — it's about meaning. It's about faith, values, systems, and vision passed down through generations. As a Kingdom entrepreneur, you are not just building a business — you are building a blueprint.

Your faith walk, your discipline, your financial decisions, and your leadership will either become stepping stones or stumbling blocks for your family. Leaving a legacy requires you to live with the end in mind and lead with intention today. When you build with legacy in focus, you stop living for survival and start planning for succession.

Whether you're the first in your family to own a business or the first to break generational curses, your obedience now is planting seeds your children's children will one day harvest. This is about more than a business — it's about building a name that carries honor in both Heaven and earth.

Don't just work for provision. Build for preservation and purpose.

Strategy Tip

Define what legacy means to you. Is it spiritual? Financial? Educational? Write a legacy letter to your children or future heirs, and create a digital legacy folder that includes:

- Business documents
- Passwords
- Wills or trusts
- Personal faith testimonies
- Final wishes and vision statements

Practical Tip

Meet with a financial advisor or estate planner to start or update your will and consider a living trust. Also, begin documenting your business's SOPs (standard operating procedures) so it can be passed down or sold.

Purpose Notes: Legacy & Wealth Tips

1. **Estate Planning:** A will and trust protect your family and business legacy.
2. **Document Processes:** SOPs ensure your business runs smoothly after you.
3. **Faith & Finances:** Share testimonies and values with heirs to strengthen spiritual legacy.

Prayer

Lord, help me build with generational vision. Let what I create today become a source of life, faith, and financial blessing for my children and their children. May my business be a vessel for Kingdom impact that outlives me. I declare that I am the blueprint for my family's breakthrough. In Jesus' name, amen.

DAY 30

Fully Surrendered, Fully Empowered

Scripture

> *"I beseech you therefore, brethren,*
> *by the mercies of God, that ye present your bodies a living sacrifice,*
> *holy, acceptable unto God, which is your reasonable service."*

— Romans 12:1

Devotion

This is your consecration moment. After all the prayers, plans, pivots, and progress — there comes a point where God says, "Now give it all back to Me." Surrender is not weakness. It is the highest form of spiritual authority.

When you surrender your business, your brand, your schedule, your revenue, and your reputation, you position yourself for divine multiplication. What you place on the altar, God breathes on. When you try to carry the weight alone, you'll burn out. But when you allow God to carry it, He lifts it higher than you ever could.

Surrender says, "God, I trust You more than my own strategy."
Surrender says, "I release control so You can release power."
Surrender is how oil flows.

You were never called to build in your own strength. You are anointed to lead, but not to lord over what belongs to God. The more you yield, the more He downloads. The more you let go, the more He establishes. And what you surrender in faith, He returns with favor.

This moment is not the conclusion — it's your Kingdom activation. Now that you've built on prayer, vision, wisdom, and strategy, God says: "Now let Me breathe on it." Fully surrendered. Fully empowered.

Strategy Tip

Schedule a "God is CEO" meeting every morning. Begin your day with prayer, a short scripture, and a moment of gratitude. Let His voice lead the agenda.

Practical Tip

Identify one area in your business where you've been forcing, striving, or stressing. Ask: *Is this my assignment or God's?* Then either **delegate** it, **automate** it, or **release** it entirely.

Purpose Notes

1. **Daily Alignment:** Begin each day connecting with God's voice through prayer and scripture.
2. **Release Burdens:** Delegate or automate tasks that hinder your peace.
3. **Expect God's Move:** Trust that surrender leads to supernatural favor and breakthrough.

Prayer

Father, I surrender it all — my business, my team, my reputation, and my results. It's not mine — it's Yours. Use it for Your glory. Let the oil of Heaven flow through every offer, email, meeting, and transaction. I remove myself from the throne and place You as CEO, Founder, Visionary, and Sustainer. Take what I've built and multiply it into a legacy that glorifies Your name. Amen.

DAY 31

Celebrating Wins God's Way

Scripture

> *"The Lord hath done great things for us; whereof we are glad."*
> — Psalm 126:3 (KJV)

Devotion

You've prayed, planned, pivoted, built, and surrendered. Now it's time to **pause and praise**. Celebration is not vanity — it's victory. In the Kingdom, celebration is a form of worship. It points back to the Source of every success.

Too often, entrepreneurs move from milestone to milestone without taking time to acknowledge what God has done. But in Scripture, God's people often built altars, feasts, and memorials to remember His faithfulness. You must do the same.

Celebrating God's way means giving Him credit **publicly**, sharing testimonies **boldly**, and encouraging others **humbly**. Your story of breakthrough, growth, and resilience could be the spark someone else needs to keep going.

You didn't just finish a devotional — you completed a Kingdom assignment. And just like the Israelites crossing the Jordan, this is your moment to plant a marker that says: *"God brought me through."*

This celebration isn't the end — it's the beginning of another level.

Strategy Tip

Celebrate with intention. Try one of the following this week:

- Host a virtual or in-person client appreciation event
- Share a testimony or "God did it" recap on social media
- Record a gratitude video or write a letter to God highlighting key wins

Let your celebration create impact.

Practical Tip

Create a "God Did It" journal or highlight reel:

- List 10 specific wins this year in your business
- Note what you learned spiritually through each one
- Include receipts or logs for any celebration expenses

Use it to both glorify God and prepare for tax season.

Purpose Notes: Faith-Fueled Celebration Tips

1. **Tell the Story:** Post a testimony online and give God the glory.
2. **Sow a Seed:** Give a "thank you" offering in honor of your wins.
3. **Honor the Team:** Celebrate staff, clients, or mentors who helped you grow.

Prayer

Lord, thank You for every win, every open door, every lesson, and every stretch. I celebrate not just the results, but the journey with You. May my testimony bring You glory and encourage others to trust You deeper. You've been faithful, and I give You all the credit. In Jesus' name, amen.

Congratulations!

You've completed *Faith to Build: 31 Days of Prayer, Purpose & Power for Kingdom Entrepreneurs*. This journey has been more than a devotional — it's a divine blueprint. Over these 31 days, you've prayed bold prayers, made strategic moves, embraced your Kingdom identity, and surrendered your vision back to the Master Builder.

But this is not the end — it's the beginning of a new level of clarity, confidence, and calling. Keep breaking chains. Keep building legacy. Keep showing up with boldness and purpose.

You are not just a business owner.
You are a **Kingdom Entrepreneur.**
And the world needs what's inside of you.

So go build—with **fire**, with **faith**, and with **freedom**.

Heaven is backing you.

Let this be your daily reminder: when **God is your CEO**, there is no limit to what you can do.

With purpose and power,
Lanice Lawrence
Author | Accountant | Kingdom Builder
Helping entrepreneurs build faith-first businesses with lasting legacy.

Faith to Build

FAITH TO BUILD DECLARATION

Speak this boldly over your life and business.

I declare that I am a Kingdom entrepreneur — chosen, anointed,
and appointed for such a time as this.
I have the mind of Christ, the wisdom of Heaven,
and the backing of God's favor.

I will build by faith, not by fear.
I will move with purpose, not pressure.
I will operate in power, not performance.

Every gift in me is activated. Every idea in me is protected.
Every seed I sow will multiply for Kingdom impact and legacy.

I am not behind — I am in divine alignment.
Doors are opening. Resources are flowing. Strategies are downloading.
Because I trust God as my CEO, I lack nothing.

I build with prayer.
I lead with integrity.
I grow with boldness.
And I finish with unstoppable joy.

This is my season to rise, to reign, and to release what God has placed
within me. In Jesus' name, **I boldly declare:**

I have faith to build—and nothing will stop me.

Amen.

Faith to Build

BONUS SECTION

Kingdom Builder's Business Toolkit

You're not just building with faith — you're building with wisdom. These practical tax, finance, and stewardship strategies will help you manage what God has entrusted to you with excellence. Let this section be your toolbox for smart, Kingdom-minded business growth.

1. Quarterly Taxes & Estimated Payments

"You don't want to build a business just to owe the IRS."

📌 If you earn income through your business, the IRS expects you to pay quarterly. Plan — don't panic.

Set aside: 25–30% of your profit (after expenses)

📅 **Quarterly Deadlines:**

- Q1: April 15
- Q2: June 15
- Q3: September 15
- Q4: January 15 (following year)

💡 **Tip:** Open a business savings account strictly for taxes. Automate monthly or bi-weekly deposits. Track net income using a bookkeeping app or spreadsheet.

2. Choosing the Right Business Structure

Your structure determines your tax burden, legal protection, and growth potential.

Structure	Pros	Cons
Sole Proprietor / DBA	Easy setup, simple taxes	No legal protection, taxed personally
LLC	Legal protection, flexible tax options	Still subject to SE tax unless elected
S-Corp	Reduces SE tax, splits income types	Requires payroll, more compliance
C-Corp	Great for scaling and investors	Double taxation, complex setup

Tip: Consult a tax pro before switching. Many save thousands by becoming an S-Corp at the right time.

3. LLC Compliance
File Your Annual Report

Most states require LLCs to file an **annual report.**

When: Usually once per year (check your state)

Cost: Varies by state ($10–$300+)

Failure to File: Can result in LLC dissolution

Tip: Mark your calendar and file on time to protect your legal standing.

4. Separate Personal & Business Finances

Blending funds creates chaos and risk.

Do This:

- Open a dedicated business bank account
- Use a business card for purchases
- Reimburse yourself with documentation

Tip: This safeguards your legal protection and keeps your records audit-ready.

5. Bookkeeping Best Practices

Stewardship starts with good records. Clean books = clear direction.

Tips:

- Use software like QuickBooks, Wave, or Xero
- Reconcile monthly
- Review profit & loss regularly
- Never mix personal and business funds

Monthly Stewardship Meeting:

Review income, plan expenses, and thank God for provision.

> *"God blesses what you manage well."*
> (Luke 16:10)

6. Business Write-Offs Every Owner Should Know

Maximize deductions legally. Steward every dollar wisely.

Examples:

- Advertising & marketing
- Business coaching
- Subscriptions (Zoom, Canva, Keeper)
- Meals (50%)
- Mileage (use MileIQ)
- Phone (business % only)
- Office supplies

Tip: Store digital receipts using Keeper, Expensify, or Google Drive. Categorize monthly.

7. Home Office Deduction

If you regularly use part of your home for business, you may qualify.

What's Deductible:

- Rent or mortgage (pro-rated)
- Utilities, internet
- Repairs to business area

Methods

- Simplified: $5/sq ft (up to 300 sq ft)
- Actual Expenses: Based on % used

Tip: Photograph your workspace and keep documentation.

8. Employing Your Child in the Business

Hiring your child is a smart way to build legacy and save on taxes.

- Ideal ages: 7–17
- Pay up to $15,000 per year tax-free (standard deduction)
- Must perform real work (filing, social media, modeling, etc.)

Tip: Paying your child through payroll allows you to deduct their wages as a business expense, reducing your taxable income. Additionally, the child can contribute to a Roth IRA, benefiting from tax-free growth.

9. Set Up a Retirement Plan

Prepare for your future while growing your legacy.

- Solo 401(k): High contribution limits for solopreneurs
- SEP IRA: Employer-only contributions
- Roth IRA: Tax-free growth

Tip: Aim to save 10–15% of net income each year.

10. Create a Board of Directors (Even as a Small Business)

A board provides guidance, accountability, and potential write-offs.

- Include trusted mentors, your spouse, or advisors
- Hold quarterly or annual meetings with minutes
- Compensate with stipends, meals, or travel (potential tax deductions)
- Tip: Maintain detailed records to satisfy IRS legitimacy requirements.

Faith to Build

Legacy Planning, Asset Protection & Financial Safeguards Worksheet

1. Legacy Planning

- Do you have a written will or living trust in place?
- Have you designated beneficiaries for all major accounts and policies?
- Have you written a legacy letter or vision for what you want to pass on — spiritually, financially, and relationally?

Legacy Vision: What legacy do you want to leave behind?

_____
_____
_____
_____
_____

2. Asset Protection

- Do you have business liability insurance, life insurance, or disability coverage?
- Are your personal and business finances properly separated?
- Do you have an operating agreement (LLC) or bylaws (corporation) in place?

Current protections in place & what needs to be added:

_____
_____
_____
_____
_____

3. Financial Safeguards

- Do you have emergency savings for both personal and business expenses?
- Are your important financial records stored securely and accessible by a trusted person?
- Have you put financial systems in place to ensure consistency and transparency (e.g., bookkeeping, budgeting)?

Legacy Planning, Asset Protection & Financial Safeguards Worksheet

Notes or updates needed to secure your finances:

_____

_____

_____

_____

_____

_____

_____

_____

_____

_____

_____

_____

_____

Legacy Vision Worksheet

1. What does legacy mean to me?

_____
_____
_____
_____

2. Who am I building this legacy for?

_____
_____
_____
_____

3. What core values do I want to pass on to my children?

_____
_____
_____
_____

4. What financial goals do I want to achieve for my family's future?

_____
_____
_____
_____

5. What spiritual or emotional inheritance do I want to leave?

_____
_____
_____
_____

6. What practical systems do I need to create or improve in my business to protect this legacy?

_____
_____
_____
_____

7. What steps will I take in the next 12 months to move closer to this legacy?

_____
_____
_____
_____

8. How will I involve my children or family in this journey?

_____
_____
_____
_____

Reflection

Legacy is not just what you leave behind, but what you build today. Commit this vision to prayer and action.

Faith to Build

Business Credit Starter Steps Worksheet

Laying the Foundation for Business Credit

> *"Through wisdom a house is built, and by understanding it is established."*
> — Proverbs 24:3

Step 1: Legal & Financial Structure

Ensure your business is properly established and separate from your personal finances.

- Register your business with your state
- Obtain your EIN (Employer Identification Number) from IRS.gov
- Open a business bank account in your business name
- Create a business email, phone number, and website (professional presence)

Step 2: Establish Business Credit Identity

These steps help lenders and vendors recognize your business as creditworthy.

- Apply for a D-U-N-S Number (free at Dun & Bradstreet: [dnb.com])
- Ensure your business address is consistent on all registrations
- Get listed in online directories (e.g., Google, Bing, Yelp if applicable)

Step 3: Begin Building with Net 30 Vendors

Start small and build credibility by using vendors that report to business credit bureaus.

Choose at least 2–3 of the following Net 30 vendors that report to D&B

Vendor Name	Reports To	Products/Services	Applied?	Approved?
Uline	D&B	Shipping, packaging supplies	[ ]	[ ]
Grainger	D&B	Tools, safety, office supplies	[ ]	[ ]
Quill	D&B	Office and janitorial supplies	[ ]	[ ]
Crown Office Supplies	D&B	Office supplies and electronics	[ ]	[ ]
Creative Analytics	D&B	Business development & marketing	[ ]	[ ]

Profit & Loss Worksheet

This financial statement is essential for managing your business and preparing your taxes. Tracking your income and expenses regularly ensures accurate records, helps you measure profitability, and simplifies tax filing. Use this worksheet to stay organized, make informed decisions, and maintain compliance—empowering you to steward your business finances with excellence and faith.

Profit & Loss Worksheet

Category	Description	Amount ($)	Notes
Income			
Sales Revenue	Income from product/service sales		
Other Income	Interest, refunds, or miscellaneous		
Total Income			
Expenses			
Cost of Goods Sold (COGS)	Direct costs of producing goods/services		
Marketing & Advertising	Ads, promotions, marketing tools		
Rent/Lease	Office or workspace rent		
Utilities	Electricity, internet, water		

Category	Description	Amount ($)	Notes
Salaries & Wages	Employee or contractor payments		
Professional Fees	Accounting, legal, consulting		
Software & Subscriptions	Business apps & tools		
Office Supplies	Stationery, printer ink, etc.		
Travel & Meals	Business trips, client meals		
Insurance	Business insurance premiums		
Taxes & Licenses	Business licenses, tax payments		
Repairs & Maintenance	Equipment or office upkeep		
Depreciation	Asset value reduction		
Miscellaneous Expenses	Other business-related expenses		
Total Expenses			

Net Profit (Loss)	Total Income - Total Expenses	

Instructions

- Fill in amounts for each income and expense category for the month.
- Use the "Notes" column for any clarifications.
- Calculate totals and subtract total expenses from total income to find your net profit or loss.
- Review monthly to track financial health and plan accordingly.

Bonus Resource

The Trifecta Blueprint for Kingdom Entrepreneurs

Protect Your Assets. Save on Taxes. Build a Legacy.
Inspired by tax attorney and CPA Mark J. Kohler

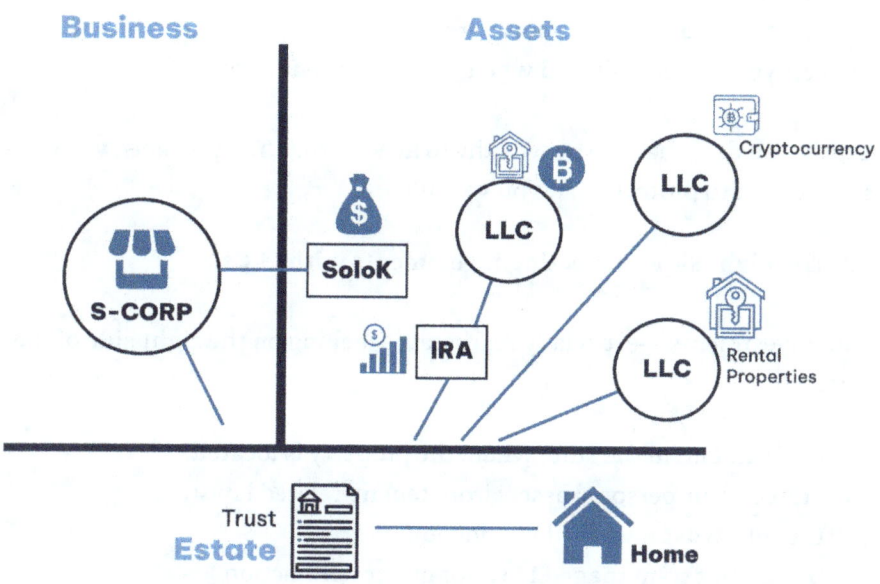

What is the Trifecta?

The Trifecta is a 3-part structure that aligns your business, personal, and investment life for maximum **tax savings, asset protection,** and **legacy planning.**

The Three Pillars

1. The Trust: Your Foundation for Legacy and Privacy

A Revocable Living Trust isn't about tax breaks — it's about organization, privacy, and protection for your family. If you own a home, have children, or care about your family's future, this is your foundation.

- Avoids probate (which costs American families over $500 billion each year)
- Keeps your estate private and out of court
- Creates a roadmap for your heirs
- Lets you decide how and when your children inherit

Truth: You don't have to be wealthy to need a trust. You just need vision — and a desire to protect what you've built.

2. The Right Side: Protecting Investments with LLCs

Your investments—especially real estate—belong on the **right side** of the Trifecta.

- Form an LLC in the state where the property is located
- Protect your personal assets from tenant-related lawsuits
- Let your **trust** own the LLC, not you
- Use **manager-managed** LLCs for greater protection

Note: LLCs are designed for **asset protection**, not tax savings. If someone tells you otherwise, they may be misinformed or offering advice that benefits their bottom line, not yours.

3. The Left Side: Your Business Engine

This is where your business—and the real tax savings—live.

If you're earning income from any business activity (full-time, part-time, side hustle), your LLC taxed as an **S Corporation** should go.

Why it matters:

By default, an LLC is taxed as a sole proprietorship, which means:

You'll pay 15.3% self-employment tax on your net profit.

What Is Net Profit?

Net profit is the money your business keeps after expenses are paid. It's what's left over after you subtract your costs from your revenue.

Formula:
Revenue – Expenses = Net Profit

Example:
If you earn $120,000 in sales and have $70,000 in business expenses:
$120,000 – $70,000 = $50,000 net profit

When to Switch to an S Corp

Once your net profit reaches $50,000, it's time to consider electing S Corp status. This allows you to split your income between salary and profit distributions — and significantly **reduce self-employment tax.**

How the S Corp Saves You

Let's say your business has $100,000 in net profit:

- You pay yourself a $40,000 salary
- You take the remaining $60,000 as a distribution

Savings: You avoid 15.3% self-employment tax on that $60K
Result: Saving $9,180 in taxes per year

What to Keep in Mind

- **You must file a separate S Corp tax return (Form 1120-S)**
  This is more complex than a Schedule C and typically costs more to prepare
- **You're required to run payroll for yourself and file quarterly payroll tax returns**
- **Staying compliant is key—but the savings and protection make it well worth it**

Disclaimer: Always consult with your CPA or tax attorney before making changes to your business structure.

Resources & References

Faith-fueled tools and practical strategies for building a business with God at the center.

Selected Scriptures

This devotional incorporates daily scriptures to anchor your spiritual and business growth. Below are some of the foundational verses featured throughout:

- Proverbs 4:7
- Habakkuk 2:2–3
- Deuteronomy 8:18
- James 2:13 (TPT)
- Jeremiah 29:11
- Matthew 6:33
- Romans 12:2
- Isaiah 48:17
- Luke 14:28
- Proverbs 13:22
- Colossians 3:23
- Psalm 90:17
- 1 Corinthians 14:40

Additional scriptures appear throughout this devotional. Unless otherwise noted, verses are quoted from the YouVersion Bible App (KJV, NLT, TPT, or NIV).

Business, Tax & Financial Tools Referenced

These are tools, frameworks, and resources mentioned throughout *Faith to Build* to help you build wisely, legally, and with legacy in mind.

- **IRS.gov**
  www.irs.gov – For EIN applications, business structure forms (e.g., Form 2553 for S-Corp election), tax publications, home office deduction guidelines, and more.
- **Mark J. Kohler's Trifecta Structure**
  A legal and financial strategy involving three parts: an operating entity (e.g., LLC/S-Corp), a holding company, and a family trust. Learn more: www.markjkohler.com
- **Dun & Bradstreet (D-U-N-S Number)**
  www.dnb.com – Essential for building business credit. Establishes your business profile and helps with vendor and lender credibility.
- **Bookkeeping Best Practices**
  Accurate bookkeeping is emphasized as the backbone of financial health and compliance. Consider working with a professional or using systems like QuickBooks or Wave.
- **Credit Repair & Business Credit Building**
  Discussed throughout the devotional. Encourages personal credit restoration, vendor credit tiers, and business credit monitoring tools like NAV and Experian Business.
- **Tax Strategy & S-Corporation Benefits**
  Introduced as part of reducing self-employment tax, maximizing deductions, and protecting your income legally through proper structuring and tax planning.

Disclaimer

This devotional is intended to provide inspiration, encouragement, and general information based on the author's personal experiences and professional background in business, finance, and faith. It is not intended to serve as legal, financial, tax, or professional advice.

Readers are strongly encouraged to seek personalized guidance from qualified professionals—such as licensed tax advisors, accountants, attorneys, or financial planners—before making decisions related to business structure, credit repair, tax strategy, or financial management.

Faith to Build

About the Author

Lanice Lawrence is a seasoned accountant, tax advisor, and business consultant with over a decade of experience empowering entrepreneurs, small business owners, and families to achieve financial clarity, growth, and lasting legacies. As the CEO and founder of Lanice Lawrence & Associates LLC, she leads a trusted firm known for providing personalized tax preparation services, strategic business advice, and expert bookkeeping services tailored to Kingdom-minded entrepreneurs.

A first-generation college graduate and native of Jamaica, Lanice brings a unique perspective shaped by her rich cultural heritage and a deep commitment to excellence. Her expertise helps clients maximize tax benefits, protect assets, and build generational wealth through smart financial planning. She blends practical financial strategies with spiritual principles, encouraging business owners to align their financial goals with their God-given purpose.

Lanice's professional journey is marked by integrity, passion, and empowerment. She serves not only as a financial expert but also as a mentor and advocate, breaking down barriers to help underrepresented entrepreneurs access the knowledge and tools they need to thrive.

Beyond her professional work, Lanice is an active minister and community leader who enjoys inspiring youth, collaborating in ministry, and spreading messages of hope and encouragement. She balances her successful career with a vibrant family life, raising four boys and two girls with her husband.

Through her work and her devotional *Faith to Build: 31 Days of Prayer, Purpose, and Power for Kingdom Entrepreneurs*, Lanice combines faith and finance to inspire others to pursue purposeful living, business success, and financial stewardship. Her dedication and expertise make her a trusted authority for entrepreneurs seeking to build not only businesses but lasting legacies grounded in faith.

Acknowledgements

To God be the glory for all that He has done. Every page of *Faith to Build* is evidence of His faithfulness, favor, and divine instruction. This devotional was birthed through prayer and obedience, and it is my honor to share what He deposited in me with Kingdom entrepreneurs everywhere.

To my loving husband — thank you for standing with me, encouraging me, and believing in the vision even when it was just an idea. Your support through long nights and early mornings means more than words can say.

To my beautiful children — this devotional is part of the legacy I am building for you. May you always walk in purpose, prayer, and bold faith.

To my parents and extended family — thank you for your consistent love, prayers, and support throughout every stage of this journey.

To my spiritual leaders and mentors—especially Pastor Paulus Taylor, First Lady Minister Patsy Taylor, and my church family at Trinity Community Church — your covering, guidance, and prayers have carried me in more ways than I can express. Thank you for cultivating a space where vision and faith can grow.

To my amazing team, including those who helped edit, design, and refine this book—thank you for your excellence, patience, and professionalism. You helped bring this vision to life with grace and precision.

To every voice who offered reviews and endorsements—your words affirmed the weight of this message and reminded me that this devotional is not just timely, but necessary. Thank you to:

- Dr. Paulus Taylor
- Minister Saneka Nelson
- Minister Kevin Lawrence
- Nickeisha Bewry-Clarke, LNHA, MHA, BSN, RN
- **Minister Carol Pusey, MDiv., BCC** – your foreword was both prophetic and powerful. Thank you for setting the tone of this book so beautifully.

To my clients and community — thank you for allowing me to serve, teach, and walk alongside you. Your growth continues to inspire mine. You are part of this testimony.

To every entrepreneur who picks up this devotional — thank you. May these words ignite your faith, clarify your purpose, and remind you that God is building something beautiful through you.

With deep gratitude,
Lanice Lawrence

www.ingramcontent.com/pod-product-compliance
Lightning Source LLC
Chambersburg PA
CBHW061942220426
43662CB00012B/1998